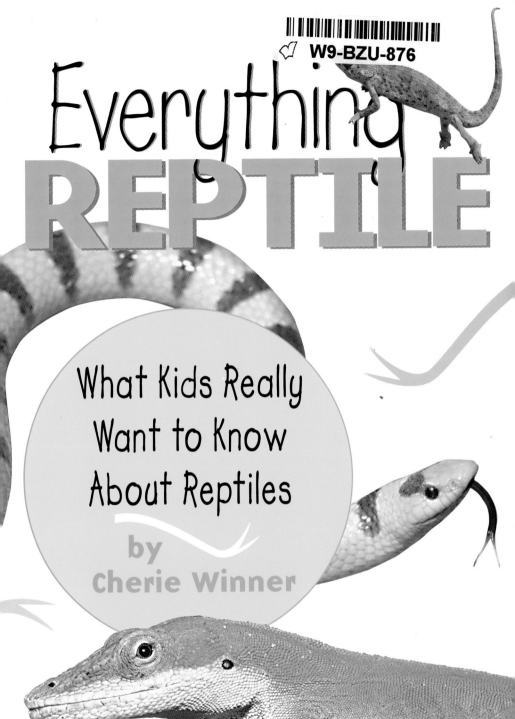

W9-BZU-876

Everything REPTILE

What Kids Really Want to Know About Reptiles

by
Cherie Winner

NorthWord Press
Minnetonka, Minnesota

Edited by Kristen McCurry
Designed by Brad Springer
Design concept by Michele Lanci-Altomare

Text © 2004 by Cherie Winner

Books for Young Readers
NorthWord Press
11571 K-Tel Drive
Minnetonka, MN 55343
www.tnkidsbooks.com

All rights reserved. No part of this work covered by the copyrights herein
may be reproduced or used in any form or by any means—graphic,
electronic, or mechanical, including photocopying, recording, or taping of
information on storage and retrieval systems—without the prior written
permission of the publisher.

Photographs © 2004 provided by:
Wolfgang Bayer/Bruce Coleman, Inc.: pp. 14-15; Mark Conlin/Seapics.com:
p. 11 top; Corel/Fotosearch.com: cover – snake, pp. 1, 13, 20, 24, 33, 37, 38,
39, 46, 52, 54, 60, 62; James Gerholdt/The Remarkable Reptiles: cover – nile
crocodile, pp. 16 top left, 31 top, 40, 44; Ross Isaacs/Seapics.com: p. 31 bottom;
Len Kaufman: p. 32; Frans Lanting/Minden Pictures: pp. 21, 49; C.C. Lockwood:
p. 23; Daniel Lyons/Bruce Coleman, Inc.: p. 45; Steve & Dave Maslowski: p. 55;
Joe McDonald/Bruce Coleman, Inc.: p. 47; Claus Meyer/Minden Pictures: p. 25;
David Northcott/Nature's Lens: p. 41; Doug Perrine/Seapics.com: pp. 27, 28-29;
Michael Sewell/Visual Pursuit: p. 11 bottom; Two-Can Publishing (Stephen
Holmes): pp. 18-19; Villoch-Visual&Written/Bruce Coleman, Inc.: p. 36; Konrad
Wothe/Minden Pictures: p. 17 bottom. All other images from Getty Images.

Library of Congress Cataloging-in-Publication Data on file

Winner, Cherie.
  Everything reptile : what kids really want to know about reptiles /
by Cherie Winner.
     p. cm.
  ISBN 1-55971-164-7 (sc) -- ISBN 1-55971-146-9 (hc)
  1. Reptiles--Juvenile literature. I. Title.

  QL644.2.W6 2004
  597.9--dc22

                              2004002887

Printed in Singapore
10 9 8 7 6 5 4 3

Acknowledgments

MANY THANKS TO THE STUDENTS AT SHELLEDY School, for their fun questions; and to Steven D. Werman, Ph.D., of Mesa State College and Pat Kuckes of the Colorado Herpetological Society, for sharing their knowledge and enthusiasm for reptiles.

Dedication

TO LINDA, PATTIE, WENDI, AND PENNY, my colleagues in composition. You rock, ladies!

—C. W.

contents

Whether climbing a tree, helping with homework, or just "hanging out," reptiles are amazing animals.

introduction

WHEN I WAS A KID, I LOVED CATCHING REPTILES in the woods near my home. I liked the way garter snakes glided over my hands, and how box turtles shut their shells whenever I got too close. Holding a lizard felt like holding a miniature dinosaur. What could be cooler than that?

Not everybody likes reptiles, though. Many people don't know much about them, and some people are downright terrified of them! Lots of the things people say about them aren't true. For instance, reptiles aren't slimy, their blood isn't cold, and they aren't out to get us. Most reptiles just want to be left alone.

When I visit schools to talk about animals, most of the kids I meet think reptiles are cool, but a little scary. They've heard stories about reptiles, and they have lots of great questions. I thought it would be fun to gather those stories and questions into a book. Who knows? If the people who don't like reptiles knew more about them, maybe they'd realize that reptiles aren't so bad after all.

What do you mean, reptiles aren't slimy?

Really, they're not! Reptile skin is covered with scales that are a lot like your fingernails. They're firm and strong, but not as hard as bone. Scales may be smooth or bumpy, depending on the species. But no matter what shape they are, they're dry. Unless a reptile has been moving in muck or swimming through seaweed, it won't be slimy at all.

Maybe you're thinking of amphibians such as frogs. Amphibians don't have scales. Instead, they are covered with slippery mucus. That feels gross to us, but mucus is very important to a frog. Like all amphibians, frogs breathe partly through their skin, and in order to do that, their skin has to be moist. If a frog's skin dries out, it will die. A nice coat of slime keeps amphibians healthy, but a reptile is happy with dry, scaly skin.

This iguana is covered with scales of different sizes, shapes, and colors. The frog has no scales at all on its smooth, slimy skin.

What are the biggest reptiles?

• • • • • • • • •

The smallest?

Reptiles come in all shapes and sizes. The longest ones are pythons and anacondas, which can be 30 feet (9.1 m) or longer. They only weigh about 500 pounds (225 kg), though. The heaviest reptiles are the leatherback sea turtles and saltwater crocs. Both of these giants weigh nearly 2,000 pounds (909 kg)—almost as much as a small car!

On the other hand, many reptiles are smaller than your pinkie finger. It's hard to say which one is THE smallest, because new species are discovered every year. Two of the smallest are lizards called the Monito gecko and the Jaragua gecko. Each is just 1.3 inches (32 mm) long—and half of that is tail! They only weigh 4/1,000 of an ounce (0.12 g), less than the weight of two Cheerios.

From huge leatherbacks to the tiniest geckos, reptiles come in many shapes and sizes.

Does "cold-blooded" mean reptiles' blood is always cold?

No, their blood is about the same temperature as their surroundings. That's why they feel cool when we touch them. Our bodies are usually warmer than the air around us. Most reptiles can't make their own heat the way we can. A few reptiles, such as some snakes, alligators, and sea turtles, can make some of their own heat, but they still depend on their surroundings for warmth.

That's why a better word for cold-blooded is "ectothermic." It means "heat from outside." A reptile warms up or cools down by moving to different places in its habitat.

On a cool morning, a lizard might sun itself on a rock, while turtles bask on a floating log. On a hot afternoon, snakes seek the shade of a burrow or bush, and alligators slide into deeper, cooler water.

Imagine what it would be like if you were ectothermic—you could bask in a sunbeam until you warmed up enough to go to school, and on cold days, you wouldn't have to get out of bed at all!

Being ectothermic has other advantages, too. A reptile doesn't need as much food as a mammal, because it doesn't use its energy to keep itself warm. That means it doesn't have to hunt as often, and it can survive longer without food.

If reptiles can't keep themselves warm, where do they go in winter?

Reptiles that live in places with cold winters find a snug burrow, or dig one themselves, and hibernate. As winter approaches, they eat a lot

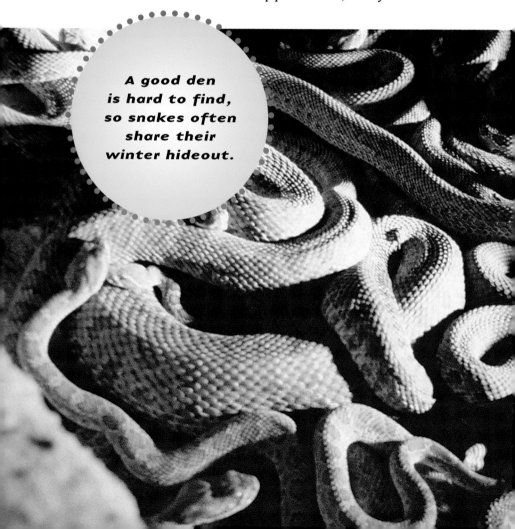

A good den is hard to find, so snakes often share their winter hideout.

and store enough fat to get them through their long sleep. Reptiles often hibernate in groups. One den can keep thousands of garter snakes cozy all winter. Some reptiles even share their den with other species. Rattlesnakes and cottonmouths will snuggle up with each other, and gopher tortoises dig burrows that are big enough for dozens of rattlesnakes, coachwhip snakes, indigo snakes, and box turtles to join them.

How many kinds of reptiles are there?

In prehistoric times, more than half a million species of reptiles roamed the Earth. Today, Earth has only about 7,000 species. Most are lizards (3,900 species) or snakes (2,500 species). The rest are turtles, alligators, crocodiles, or two unusual kinds of reptiles most people have never heard of, amphisbaenians and tuataras.

Amphisbaenians look so much like worms that they are called "worm lizards." They live underground and hardly ever come to the surface. Tuataras are sometimes called "living fossils." Their ancestors thrived all over the world 200 million years ago. Only two species are still alive today. They live on islands in New Zealand. As you can see, tuataras look a lot like iguanas. They grow up to 2 feet (61 cm) long and have a row of spines down their back. They also have a "third eye" in the middle of the forehead. This eye can't see specific things, but it can sense lights and shadows.

Were dinosaurs reptiles?

Probably, but not everyone agrees. Most biologists think that dinosaurs were a group of reptiles, like the lizard and turtle groups today. However, they weren't the only group of reptiles alive at the time. Many others roamed the Earth back then. But some biologists think dinosaurs were very different from other reptiles—so different that they weren't reptiles at all.

The closest relatives of dinosaurs we see today are the birds. Some people even think that birds are reptiles—reptiles with feathers!

There's a lot yet to figure out about reptiles and dinosaurs. Maybe you will help answer these questions.

Are birds reptiles? Some people think so!

Aren't salamanders reptiles?

Salamanders look so much like lizards that a lot of people think they're the same thing. They are very different, though. Like other reptiles, lizards have scales and breathe through lungs. Their eggs are protected by a leathery shell. Salamanders, like frogs, are amphibians. They have slimy skin rather than scales, and they breathe through gills when they are young. Most of them lose their gills and breathe through lungs when they grow up. Their eggs are covered with clear jelly and do not have a shell.

Do reptiles lay eggs?

All female reptiles *make* eggs, but not all reptiles *lay* eggs. How's that for a confusing answer? Most reptiles lay their eggs in nests of sand or twigs and the babies hatch there. However, in some lizards and snakes, the mother incubates her eggs within her body. The eggs hatch while they're still inside the mother, and the babies crawl out. This is called "live birth."

Do reptiles take care of their babies?

Most reptiles don't take care of their young the way mammals or birds do. A mother reptile digs a burrow or makes a nest where her eggs or new babies will be hidden from predators such as birds and coyotes. But most reptile moms don't stay near the nest. Their babies are on their own as soon as they hatch or are born.

A few species do more to help their young. The king cobra mother makes a nest out of rotting leaves. It's like a little compost pile. As the leaves decay, they heat up and help incubate her eggs. The cobra mom stays near the nest and chases away intruders who might want to eat her eggs.

Alligators and crocodiles are the best reptile parents of all. They act more like birds than like other reptiles. They build a strong nest out of twigs, or bury their eggs in damp soil. When it's time for an egg to hatch, the baby inside squeaks, grunts, and scratches the shell with its egg tooth. This is a small spine on the front of its jaw that

This baby alligator has the safest seat in the pond—its mother's mouth!

will disappear soon after hatching. When the mother hears her babies trying to hatch, she comes to help. She digs through the soil to reach the eggs. Then she picks them up and rolls them around in her huge mouth. That tears open the leathery shells so the babies can come out. The mother carries her little ones to a quiet pool of water and lets them go. In some species the father carries the babies, too.

Young gators and crocs may stay near their parents for a year or more. The parents probably don't feed them, but the young clean up leftovers from their parents' meals.

What do reptiles eat?

Many reptiles are herbivores, or plant-eaters. Big land turtles eat fruit and leaves, and the marine iguanas on the Galapagos Islands just love seaweed. Other reptiles are carnivores, or meat-eaters. What prey they eat depends on where they live and how big they are. Reptiles that spend a lot of time in the water eat fish, frogs, crabs, or other aquatic creatures. Reptiles on land eat insects, eggs, rodents— just about anything they can catch. Bigger reptiles eat bigger prey. A Komodo dragon, which is a monitor lizard nearly as big as a tiger, stalks and kills large mammals much like a tiger does. A Komodo can even kill an adult water buffalo!

Do other animals eat reptiles?

Oh, yes. Reptiles get eaten by many kinds of animals, including birds, coyotes, fish, and other reptiles. Alligators especially like the taste of turtle, and some hawks would starve if they couldn't find enough snakes to eat.

Do reptiles ever eat people?

Actually, we are more likely to eat reptiles than they are to eat us. People eat rattlesnake meat, lizard legs, turtle soup, and alligator tails, among other reptilian dishes. In Central America, iguanas are so popular as a food that they are called *gallina de palo*—"chicken of the tree."

Only a few reptiles purposely hunt humans. People who live near Nile crocodiles and large pythons have learned to watch out for these deadly creatures.

Most reptiles won't attack a person unless the person is trying to catch or kill them. Alligators sometimes grab a child or a dog that comes into their territory, especially in places where people have left food out for the alligators. When that happens, the gators lose their natural fear of humans. Instead of swimming away when they see a person, they might think the person is another free meal.

Humans even eat endangered species sometimes. These eggs in a market in Costa Rica came from olive ridley sea turtle nests.

Why not get rid of the alligators if people live nearby?

Without alligators, many fish and other aquatic animals would die. Gators keep their habitat healthy by scooping out deep holes on the

This alligator might look slow and sleepy, but if it spots a meal it will move lightning-fast.

bottoms of ponds. Even if the rest of the pond dries up in summer, gator holes will still have water in them. Fish, frogs, and turtles find refuge there until rain fills the pond again.

Besides, the alligators didn't come into our territory. We came into theirs. People and alligators can live near each other, if people don't crowd the gators—or feed them.

What's the difference between an alligator and a crocodile?

Look at their mouths—from a safe distance, of course! When an alligator's mouth is closed, you can't see most of its lower teeth. When a crocodile's mouth is closed, you can see several lower teeth, including a long one near the front that fits into a notch on the outside of the upper jaw.

Another difference is that crocodiles have a spot on each belly scale that can sense vibrations in the water. Alligators have those spots around the jaws, but nowhere else. Since it's a little dangerous to get a close look at their bellies, it's easier to look at their mouths.

An alligator shows mostly upper teeth when its mouth is closed. A crocodile shows upper and lower teeth. One lower tooth is so big it makes a dent in the upper jaw.

I saw a picture of a man wrestling an alligator. Isn't an alligator a lot stronger than a person?

Alligators are incredibly strong. They can shut their jaws hard enough to crush a deer with one chomp. But the muscles they use to *open* their mouths are so weak that a strong person can hold the jaws shut with one hand. An alligator wrestler has to be very careful, though. If the alligator thrashes around and the wrestler loses his grip—c-r-r-runch!

Turtles must be strong, too, to carry those shells. How much does a turtle shell weigh?

A turtle shell is probably lighter than you'd think. It's made of two layers, an outer layer of scales, and an inner layer of bones. In most turtles, the bones are very thin. In large turtles such as the Galapagos tortoise, the bones are thicker, but they contain hollow spaces so the shell is light enough for the tortoise to carry.

Leatherback sea turtles and softshell turtles don't have scales on their shells. Instead, their shell bones are covered by thick, leathery skin. They still have scales on their legs and head, though.

How much room do turtles have inside their shell?

Not much. Some turtles can't even fit their head inside their shell. Others draw the head straight back into the shell, or tuck it in sideways. Either way, it's a tight fit—so tight that a turtle can't breathe while its head and legs are inside the shell. Its lungs don't have room to move!

Are all turtles slow?

Yes, on land, turtles are pokey. At top speed, a box turtle might be able to go two or three city blocks in an hour. Don't let his walking speed fool you, though. If you wave a finger in front of him, he can chomp down on it in a flash!

Turtles are much faster in the water than on land. Some freshwater turtles swim faster than fish. Sea turtles migrate hundreds or thousands of miles (kilometers) within a few weeks, so they have great endurance as well as speed.

Can sea turtles breathe underwater?

Believe it or not, they can—not well enough to stay underwater forever, but they don't have to come up for air very often. Unlike fish, they don't have gills. Instead, they take in oxygen through their skin, their throat, and an opening under the tail called the cloaca.

How can a snake swallow something bigger than its head?

Maybe you've heard that a snake can make its lower jaw drop away from its upper jaw when it tackles a large meal. That's true, but it's only part of the story. The lower jaw also spreads apart! The left side of the chin separates from the right side. Most of the other bones in a snake's skull also move, so the whole head changes shape when a snake eats.

The skull isn't the only part of a snake that changes to fit around large prey. Their ribs spread out and their gut stretches to several times its normal size. If you think you're full after Thanksgiving dinner, take a look at a one-inch-thick (2.5 cm) snake that's just swallowed a two-inch-thick (5 cm) meal!

How can I tell if a snake is dangerous?

The best way is to know what kinds of snakes you are likely to meet, what the dangerous ones look like, and where they like to hang out. In the United States, only a few species are dangerous to humans. Most of them, including rattlesnakes, copperheads, and water moccasins, have a triangular head rather than a narrow head.

These rattlesnakes have the triangular head seen on most venomous snakes in North America.

You'd have a lot more to worry about in Australia, where almost half of the snake species have deadly venom.

When you're walking in snake territory, watch where you step. Don't put your hand down a hole or in a brush pile where a snake might be resting. Most snakes won't come after you. But if you surprise them, corner them, or threaten their nest, they will strike. To be totally safe, if you see a snake, leave it alone. Chances are, the snake is more afraid of you than you are of it.

Can you spot the Massasauga rattlesnake in this picture?

After coiling around a rattlesnake, a large king snake gets ready to chomp down.

Do snakes ever die from their own poison?

Yes! A snake has no problem carrying its own venom inside glands in its mouth, or swallowing prey that it killed with venom. But if a snake bites itself, it may die. That happens sometimes when snakes are captured and put under a lot of stress.

Some snakes are immune to other snakes' venom. For example, king snakes hunt and eat rattlesnakes. Rattlers seem to know that their venom doesn't work against this enemy. If a king snake attacks a rattler, the rattler tries to wrestle it down but usually doesn't try to bite it.

I heard that a snake is just a lizard without legs. Is that true?

Actually, snakes are more like lizards without ears. Lizards hear much the same way we do. They have ear holes on the sides of the head, and eardrums for sensing sounds through the air. Snakes don't have ear holes or eardrums. Instead of hearing sounds that come through the air, they sense vibrations that come through the ground.

Snakes also don't have eyelids they can blink with, as most lizards do. Instead, snakes have a clear scale called a spectacle, or eye cap, over each eye.

As for snakes being lizards without legs, well, there really are lizards that don't have legs. They're called (what else?) legless lizards. They live under fallen leaves, or in narrow tunnels they dig with their tough snouts.

There also are a few snakes that have vestigial, or remnant, legs. Pythons and boas, for example, have short stubs where their ancestors had hind legs.

They're both green, but the anole lizard (below) can hear you talk, and the green snake (left) will never blink.

Do all reptiles shed their skin the way snakes do?

As a snake grows, a brand-new set of scales forms underneath the old one. When the new scales are ready, the old ones fall off. They come off all in one piece, so we can see that the snake is shedding its whole skin. Lizards, tuataras, and amphisbaenians also shed their whole skin, but it comes off in patches instead of in one piece. They shed several times every year.

Turtles, alligators, and crocodiles do it differently. Their old scales stay attached to the new scales. Over time, the old scales wear down. Some of them eventually fall off, one at a time. Others stay attached for the animal's whole life.

This garter snake slithers out of its old skin (above). A shedding snake loses every old scale, including the eyecap over each eye.

I saw a lizard that looked like it was doing push-ups. Was it exercising?

No, it was showing off. Male lizards often do "push-ups" to make themselves look bigger and to display the bright colors on their throat or belly. That tells females they would make a good mate, and tells other males to stay away.

Can lizards walk on water?

No, but some can run on water. The basilisk lizard of Central and South America stands up and runs on its hind legs when it needs to move in a hurry. A basilisk can even run across ponds. It doesn't fall in because its toes have flaps of skin that work like paddles, and it moves quickly. If it slows down to a walk, it will fall in. Then the basilisk will have to swim, which it does by wiggling its whole body back and forth.

Do "flying lizards" really fly?

Lizards don't fly, but some of them parachute and a few are great gliders. They can't lift themselves into the air, so they have to start from a high place, such as a tree branch, that they reach by climbing.

Some "gliding geckos" have webbed feet and flaps of skin along their sides and tail. When they drop out of a tree, they spread their toes and skin flaps and drift downward like a skydiver with an open parachute.

A "flying lizard" is built more like an umbrella. It has long ribs that fold down along its sides when the lizard is standing. When the lizard jumps off a tree, his ribs fan out and the skin between them unfolds, like the cloth of an umbrella opening up. The lizard can't go higher than he started, but he can glide several dozen yards (meters), and he can steer with his tail and legs.

This flying lizard from Borneo glides by unfolding its ribs to spread out the skin flaps along its sides.

Can all lizards lose their tail and grow it back again?

• • • • • • • • • •

Can they do it more than once?

Not all lizards do this, but many species can drop part of their tail if a predator comes after them. The predator doesn't even have to grab the tail; it just falls off. The tail keeps wiggling for a

Some lizards, including geckos like these, can lose part of their tail—and grow it back.

few minutes. Sometimes the predator pounces on the wiggling tail, and the lizard gets away. Sometimes the predator isn't fooled, and it catches the lizard anyway.

A lizard's tail can break off at several places along its length. The break is very clean, with hardly any bleeding. Later, the tail re-grows from the stump. You can usually tell if a lizard's tail has regenerated. The new part has a different pattern or color than the old part, and it may look smaller than it should be.

A lizard can lose and re-grow its tail many times, but each time, the tail breaks off closer to the body. That means there's more to grow back.

That's a big drain on the lizard. It takes a lot of energy to grow a tail, and until the tail is full size again, it's not much good for balance or steering.

Do all lizards change their color to blend in with their surroundings?

Most lizards don't change their color at all. But some, such as African chameleons, are great at matching the colors around them. When they're sitting on leaves, they will be green, but if they move to a tree trunk, they will turn brown.

Other lizards, such as the anoles in the southeastern United States, change color depending on the weather. When it's warm, anoles are bright green, and in cool weather, they're more brown. Anoles also change color when they defend their territory or advertise for a mate.

Anoles (left) change color with the weather. Chameleons (this page) match the color and pattern of their surroundings.

Is it true that lizards can shoot blood out of their eyeballs?

This sounds like a wild story somebody just made up, but it's true. Some horned lizards in the southwestern United States can shoot blood from their eyes. When the lizard is cornered by a predator, or a person, it closes the veins that carry

blood out of its head back into the body. Blood keeps flowing into the head, but it can't flow out again. Blood vessels in the eye sockets fill up until they burst, squirting blood up to 4 feet (1.2 m) away. That startles the predator, and sometimes even hits him in the eyes. This gives the horned lizard a chance to scurry away.

Horned lizards may look scary, but this tactic shows how harmless they are. They would rather shoot blood out of their eyes than get caught by you!

If reptiles are so scared of us, how come so many people are afraid of them?

Good question. We should be scared of reptiles that are truly dangerous, but why be afraid of a tiny ringneck snake or a colorful gecko?

Some people fear reptiles because someone once hid a lizard in their jacket or waved a snake near their face. It wasn't the reptile's fault, but the reptile got the blame for an unpleasant experience.

Few people are scared of turtles, maybe because turtles move so slowly. Even if they were dangerous, we could easily get out of their way. But snakes and lizards move so fast we can't keep track of them. They hang out in hidden places among rocks or leaves, almost as if they are waiting for us to walk by. Many lizards have sharp spines, or eyes that swivel around to look in every direction. Snakes flick out their weird-looking forked tongues.

Hollywood movies show giant reptiles devouring people, cars, and houses.

Maybe people fear reptiles because they don't know about the good things reptiles do, like eating insects and rodents, providing food for other wildlife, and creating places where other animals can live. There's a lot to like about reptiles!

And besides, reptiles are just plain cool. Who would believe that a snake can poison itself, sea turtles breathe through their butts, and lizards squirt blood out of their eyes? With reptiles, the truth is often even more amazing than the tall tales.

A carpet python prowls for dinner,
a box turtle meets a new friend, and
iguanas bask on a sunny beach.

tall tales about reptiles

Tortoises live for hundreds of years.

We don't know if this is true or not.
Tortoises, especially the really big ones like
the Galapagos tortoise, live 50 years or longer. That's
a long life compared to most other animals. But tales
of them living for centuries may not be true. The
problem is, we don't have good records about
individual tortoises. A big tortoise might look a lot
older than it really is. Even in captivity, where they
usually live longer than they would in the wild, only a
few tortoises reach their 75th birthday.

You can tell how old a rattlesnake is by counting the number of rattles on its tail.

Absolutely false! The number of rattles on a
rattlesnake's tail depends on how much the snake eats
and how fast it grows. In a year with a long summer

and plenty of prey, a rattler might grow four or five new rattles. At the same time, its old rattles get worn down and fall off. You can't learn much of anything about a rattlesnake by counting its rattles.

If I flush a baby alligator down the toilet, it will live in the sewers.

If you flush an alligator down the toilet, all you'll get is trouble. The gator will probably clog the plumbing, and it won't survive long. Alligators often live in swamps, but they like *clean* swamps. Sewage will kill them. If you have a baby alligator that's getting too big to keep as a pet, don't flush it or let it loose in a pond. Call your state's wildlife department and ask for help finding a new home for the animal.

Better yet, don't get an alligator as a pet in the first place. Many reptiles look cute when they're small. But when a gator outgrows the bathtub or an iguana gets bigger than your cocker spaniel, they're not so cute any more.

resources

BOOKS

ALDERTON, DAVID. Crocodiles and Alligators of the World. New York: Sterling Publishing Company, 1998.

BADGER, DAVID and JOHN NETHERTON. Lizards: A Natural History of Some Uncommon Creatures. Stillwater, MN: Voyageur Press, 2002.

BROWN, DAVID E. and NEIL B. CARMONY. Gila Monster: Facts and Folklore of America's Aztec Lizard. Salt Lake City: The University of Utah Press, 1999.

COGGER, HAROLD G. and RICHARD G. ZWEIFEL, eds. Reptiles & Amphibians. New York: SMITHMARK Publishers Inc., 1992.

COOPER, PAULETTE. 277 Secrets Your Snake Wants You to Know: Unusual and Useful Information for Snake Owners and Snake Lovers. Berkeley: Ten Speed Press, 1999.

GIBBONS, WHIT. Their Blood Runs Cold. Tuscaloosa, AL: The University of Alabama Press, 1983.

LOCKWOOD, C.C. The Alligator Book. Baton Rouge: Louisiana State University Press, 2000.

ORENSTEIN, RONALD. Turtles, Tortoises, and Terrapins: Survivors in Armor. Toronto: Firefly Books, 2001.

RICCIUTI, ED. The Snake Almanac. New York: The Lyons Press, 2001.

WEB SITES

www.pbs.org/wnet/nature/victims/
Visit this page to learn about making medicines from venom, a man who has been bitten by venomous snakes more than 300 times, and rattlesnake roundups.

www.pbs.org/wnet/nature/reptiles/
This page will tell you something new about every kind of reptile. You can even download reptile "wallpaper" for your computer screen.

www.cccturtle.org/sat1.htm
At this site, you'll meet sea turtles that carry radio transmitters so biologists can track them on their migrations. Trace their travels on your own map of the world's oceans.

www.naturenorth.com/spring/
This site shows you what happens when hibernating garter snakes come out of their dens in spring. It also has tips for keeping garter snakes as classroom pets. Make sure your teacher sees this!

http://octopus.gma.org/turtles/
On this page from the Gulf of Maine Aquarium, you can read about snapping turtles, loggerheads, and other kinds of turtles.

http://www.flmnh.ufl.edu/natsci/herpetology/brittoncrocs/ cbd-faq.htm
This cool site covers just about everything you'd ever want to know about crocodiles, alligators, and their relatives.

http://www.sdnhm.org/exhibits/reptiles/index.html
This page from the San Diego Natural History Museum includes a name-the-reptile game and a dinosaur coloring book you can make yourself.

http://dmoz.org/Kids_and_Teens/School_Time/Science/ Living_Things/Animals/Reptiles_and_Amphibians/Reptiles/
This page has links to dozens more sites on all kinds of reptiles. It's a great place to get started if you want to find out Everything Reptile!

www.parcplace.org/education/sparc/index.htm
Hosted by Student Partners in Amphibian and Reptile Conservation, this page shows how kids around the country have created reptile habitats, led reptile walks, and done other fun projects with reptiles.

www.herpdigest.org/
At this Web site you can sign up to receive an e-mail newsletter about reptiles and amphibians.

About the Author

CHERIE WINNER WRITES BOOKS AND ARTICLES FOR children and adults. Her favorite subjects are animals and plants, and the people who study them. Several of her books have been named Outstanding Science Trade Books for Children. Dr. Winner has taught college classes, done research on salamanders, and worked as a newspaper reporter. Nowadays, when she isn't writing about nature, she enjoys creating mini-habitats in her yard to attract insects, spiders, snakes, and birds. This puzzles her dog Sheba and cat Smudge, but they are good sports about it.

Wendi Silvano

Do you have questions about other animals? We want to hear from you! E-mail us at **kidsfaqs@tnkidsbooks.com**
For more details, log on to **www.tnkidsbooks.com**